ROXIE BERRY

WOMAN OF COLOR FROM DIFFERENT SHADES OF COLOR.

ISBN: 978-1-965082-32-4
Publishing By: DemiCo National, LLC
www.DemiCoNational.com

Color of The Wind

The color of smooth enhanced beauty. The voice carries silky words that resemble the river flows of hope.

The creation of navigating dreams of human nature. The characteristics that develop the cycle of our personal growth.

AFRO

Afro is the symbol of natural beauty, the root of the nation that holds power with the tip of being headstrong. Blackness of our pride and ambition, the moment,movement, and memories celebrate our heritage.The power to enhance the unity of love. The texture of hair long, short, curling,cornrow, dreadlock, and nappy. Define the beauty of lovely essence. The perfection of wisdom that goes beyond the flesh.
Ambition
Free
Reach
Opportunity.

ALABAMA SISTER

The home away from home for me was watching as time drifted apart. The memories I kept alive there were moments that were disasters being discovered. It is like unlocking the key in the door. What was there on the other side of that door was a whole new world that I had to grab, but I was willing to ride the waves of opportunity.

SISTERHOOD WOMAN OF COLOR FROM DIFFERENT SHADES OF COLOR

There are lessons that we don't see coming. Learning as we go along the rollcoster of life has been a wake up call. Being resilient puts things in perspective, knowing your purpose with a carefree spirit.

FAMILY

My sister,
who had accomplished and accepted
that no mountain, wasn't hard for her
to climb. She never one discouraged
herself from learning and master the
art of determination.

My brother,
The music flowed a beat and a tune
the mellow of the atmosphere the
range how music enter the eternal
soul of calm and peace. Beat at your
own drum.

My children,
The love of struggle and putting our
lives back together again.The eyes of
a lifetime of learning and lessons that
will always be within the test of time.

TEACHERS

Teachers are an inspiration to the tunnel vision of love. Don't ever dim your light. The shade and shadow beautifully shower the great transformation in a heartbeat of excellence.

Holding back the teardrops of rivers cast every bubble with a transpire message of courage.

CRISIS

How many times have you come across a crisis? Did you stop yourself from pursuing your purpose? The birth name hold your right as a woman, the name that was given to your intelligence, limelight, beauty of mastering the art of many blessings that are being stored in your life.

CLASS OF 1995

It was 30 years ago when I was a graduate of A.C. FLora High School. Fly Falcon Fly! Looking back over my life, do you really think I knew where life was going to land? Apparently, not. It was all new to me. A new state, new friends, and a new life all in a nutshell. It wasn't the laugh, it was the teardrop that formed hate toward myself. In a world lost without loving yourself you fall for the yoki dope. No kinds of passion or purpose for life. I did give school a try the first time around and I couldn't grasp on to the lesson until years later.

GRIEVING MOTHER

There isn't a time limit on being grief stricken. Mental health turns into mental illness, sadness, and depression of losing a loved one. The recurring episode that plays in our mind sane and insane wanting to hear their voice again. The saying goes, "You can't walk in nobody's shoes or tell people how to grieve. It's a different shade of grieving as the season unfolds hand in hand. Keep thriving for your family members; they're the one looking down upon you. Don't be discouraged. Your best is still yet to come. We don't know the hour or day. Make. everyday count not like it your very last. Like it's your very first time creating memories, enjoy the beautiful blessings and keep their legacy alive.

MOTHERLESS DAUGHTER

Dry your eyes my child.
Do you remember the
lesson that was taught
throughout your
childhood? A lesson that
carried you into your
womanhood?

WOMANHOOD

The choice of reasons, resources, and research is the identity of our ethical results, independent and codependent. How could one regret their past of resources and the revolution of their personal experience.

DENIAL

Is the worst-case scenario
knowing time doesn't stop for
anyone. Watering yourself as a
plant feeds yourself some
nutrients and grows a long,
healthy life. You're the root of your
foundation. Deeper into the soil
deeper, the work will begin
enabling your need, and want.

50/50

50/50 is when my childhood
got split up in-between two
states that was enough for me.
It was all or nothing and giving
up wasn't an option. I do not
follow the 50/50 rule
somewhere in between you will
be lacking something.There
isn't no need for me to make
something look perfect when it
is not.

CRIME OF PASSION

Crime is a passion when you are at fault for loving someone who can't be in your eternity presence. No judgment, something wasn't meant to be pushed and pulled.The readjustment of life seeing what was left behind to make anew.

RAIN

The reminisce had me lost in
the whirlwind of a whirlpool just
for a moment toxicity love.
Falling for companionship that
seems to vanish only for a
minute in time.

The pouring rains of tears drop
dripped, making puddles that
had me confused. One day,
the sun was going to shine.

YOUNG AT HEART

Once in a lifetime journey you only be a teenager one time. The first crush. The first love. The first everything. Life transformation coming full circle. Lifestyles have a way of having a detour into another destination.

Explore all options of your existence. Vivid memories of the unthinking that came to life is a scene from a movie. I have been explaining myself for the longer. Busted of energy so vibrant the world is your oyster.

REGRET

What is a regret not accepted and accomplished a dreams. As long as you have breath in your body, it shouldn't be anything big and small that you can not handle.

Why complain about not doing anything great for yourself. Never forget you did something great. You live in your truth if it was only for a moment. You were a lesson of many seasons, the root that kept growing without actually being seen.

LIVING IN GRIEF

Life will transform you in more ways than one that you didn't see coming.You have the strength to keep thriving for yourself as well as your children.Time will not become a statue to transpire somebody else in their moments of grief.

Keep persevering, you have your congratulations in order. Nothing comes easy. If it did you wouldn't have a story to tell or a title to introduce.

FAREWELL
NEVER GOODBYE

The saddest day is walking across the stage in a new life. Friends separated once again and you've tried to save all the phone numbers. Being happy at that very moment in time. I didn't want life to stop, but time kept moving forward. The hugs turn into not letting go- hold on a little while longer. The goodbye seems like Hello, how are you doing, The farewells seem like this is your first time at this school. The walk seems unpredictable. A whole new world I had to conquer my very own again. Life started moving fast without a pause button.

DEDICATION

I dedicate this book to the many women who came into my life over 35 years ago. Some that have gone on to glory, but their legacy remains close to our eternal souls through traumatized trauma, tragedy, test, testimony, and triumphant.

As you read the many poems, please remember that women of color wear many different styles, textures, and techniques. As you explore the many colors the shade doesn't ever go away.

−ROXIE

THANK YOU FOR YOUR SUPPORT

This book wouldn't be possible without the women, from all walks of life who put me in my place when I was doing wrong. They're a God sent to many accomplishments that are still coming into their lives.